GÚNA NUA THEATRE COMPANY AN

BY ELAINE MURPHY

AMBER	Sarah Greene
LORRAINE	Hilda Fay
KAY	Anita Reeves

Director	Paul Meade
Designer	Alice Butler
Lighting Designer	Mark Galione
Music and Sound Designer	Carl Kennedy
AV Designer	Jack Phelan
Production Manager	Mike Burke / Mark Galione
Stage Director	Marella Boschi
Photography	Peter Houlihan and Futoshi Sakauchi
Set Construction	Ian Thompson

Gúna Nua Theatre Company

ARTISTIC DIRECTOR	Paul Meade
GENERAL MANAGER	John O'Brien

Civic Theatre

ARTISTIC DIRECTOR	Bríd Dukes
GENERAL MANAGER	Kerry Hendley

Little Gem was premiered in the United States by the
Carol Tambor Theatrical Foundation, with the support of Culture Ireland, as part of the
Best of Edinburgh Award, 5 January 2010, at The Flea Theatre, New York City.

Little Gem premiered at the Dublin Fringe Festival 2008,
with Anita Reeves as Kay, Hilda Fay as Lorraine and Aoife Duffin as Amber.

First performed in the UK at Traverse Theatre, Edinburgh,on Thursday 6 August 2009,
as part of the 2009 Edinburgh Festival Fringe, with cast as above.

CAST BIOGRAPHIES

Hilda Fay (*Lorraine*) Hilda graduated from the Samuel Beckett Centre, Trinity College Dublin. Her theatre work includes: *The Vagina Monologues*, *The Woman Who Walked into Doors*, *Fontamara*, *Green*, *Kiss 'n' Tell*, *Aladdin*, *Cinderella*, *Sinbad*, *An Feilican Fan*, *Trojan Women*. Her film and television work includes: *Finbar's Class*, *Ordinary Decent Criminal*, *Saltwater*, *Though the Sky Falls*, *Recoil*, *On the Street Where She Lives*, *Proof*, *Prosperity*, *The Clinic*, *Whistleblower*. She is mostly recognised for playing Tracey for the last seven years in RTÉ's *Fair City*. Hilda most recently appeared in *The Playboy of the Western World* at the Abbey Theatre. She was awarded the joint Best Actress Award for *Little Gem* in the Dublin Fringe Festival 2008. Hilda has also been nominated for Best Supporting Actress for *Whistleblower* (2009), and received the Best Actress nomination for *Fair City* in the 2009 TV Now Awards.

Sarah Greene (*Amber*) Sarah is a graduate of the full-time professional acting course at the Gaiety School of Acting, Dublin. Theatre credits include *The Empress of India*, *The Year of the Hiker*, *The Playboy of the Western World* (Druid Theatre). Sarah also appeared to much acclaim as Cactus in Gina Moxley's play *Danti Dan* (Galloglass Theatre Company) and more recently in *The Death of Harry Leon* (Ouroboros Theatre Company). Her film and television work includes: *RAW* (Season Two, Octagon/RTÉ), *Bachelor's Walk Christmas Special*, *Den Tots*, *Bandstand*, *Speed Dating* (RTÉ). Sarah appeared as Imelda in *Eden*, the feature film based on Eugene O'Brien's award-winning play of the same name (Samson/RTÉ). She is currently appearing as Cathleen in the Canadian-Irish feature film *Love and Savagery* (Morag Loves Company, Subotica and Park Ex Pictures) in festivals across North America. Sarah most recently completed filming on the new feature film *The Guard*, written and directed by John McDonagh and starring Brendan Gleeson and Don Cheadle and due for release in 2010.

Anita Reeves (*Kay*) Anita's most recent appearance was at the Abbey Theatre as the Nurse in *Romeo and Juliet*. Other theatre work includes: *Sweeney Todd* (Gate Theatre); *The Pirates of Penzance*, *A Life* (Olympia Theatre); *Les Misérables* (Point Theatre); *Shirley Valentine* (Tivoli Theatre); *She Stoops to Conquer*, *The Rivals*, *The Shaughraun*, *Da*, *Dancing at Lughnasa* (Abbey Theatre, Dublin); *Juno and the Paycock* (Gaiety Theatre); *HMS Pinafore* (Old Vic, London); *The Plough and the Stars* (Garrick Theatre); *The Cripple of Inishmaan* (National Theatre); *Naked* (Almeida and Playhouse Theatres). She created the role of Maggie in the original production of *Dancing at Lughnasa* at the National Theatre and the Phoenix Theatre. Film work includes: *Angel*, *Into the West*, *Ballroom of Romance*, *The Miracle*, *Talk of Angels*, *Fools of Fortune*, *Scarlett*, *The Butcher Boy*, *The American*, *Adam & Paul*, *Alarm*.

PRODUCTION TEAM BIOGRAPHIES

Marella Boschi (Stage Director) Marella arrived in Ireland from Italy in 1993. After graduating in the Inchicore VEC College Stagecraft course, she has been employed full-time in theatre, mainly as a stage manager. She has also operated sound and lights, and occasionally designed costumes and sets. She has toured Ireland many times, as well as London, Belgium, and Poland, with various different shows, working with many theatres and theatre companies, including The Abbey, National Theatre, Second Age, Axis Productions, Calypso, Fishamble and Common Currency. She has also worked on Opera Ireland and the Wexford Opera Festival. In 2001, Marella toured Ireland as Stage Director for the monologue she had translated from Italian into English, *1900 The Pianist on the Ocean*.

Mike Burke (Production Manager) Mike is based in Limerick and worked on many Island Theatre Company productions as Stage/Production Manager, and on set construction. He is a co-founder of Limerick's new theatre company, Bottom Dog Theatre. Other companies Mike has worked with include: Reduced Shakespeare Company (USA), An Grianan (Letterkenny), Yew Tree Theatre (Mayo), Ouroboros Theatre Company (Dublin), Daghdha Dance Company (Limerick), Gallowglass Theatre Company (Clonmel), Production Partnership Company (London), Gúna Nua Theatre Company (Dublin), Joan Sheehy Productions and Limerick Theatre Hub. In addition to theatre, Mike also works on TV productions as Construction Manager for such series as *Killinaskully*. In film, he has worked as Art Assistant on *True North* (Carlingfort Films), *Eden* (Samson Films); as Assistant Art Director on *The Ballad of Kid Kanturk* (Wildfire Films); and most recently on the pilot episode of Pat Short's *Mattie*.

Alice Butler (Designer) Before leaving Dublin to study at the Motley Theatre Design course in London, Alice assisted Cisato Yoshimi on her design for Ulick O'Connor's *Submarine*, directed by Caroline Fitzgerald. After finishing the course, which ended with an exhibition at the National Theatre, London, Alice worked as set builder and costume maker for *Reverence; A Tale of Abelard and Eloise* at the Southwark Playhouse in the vaults under London Bridge. She then went on to design set and costumes for *One in Five* by Penelope Skinner at the King's Head Theatre, and *The Slow Sword*, a new Russian play directed by Noah Birksted-Breen for Sputnik Theatre Company at the Old Red Lion, both in Angel, North London. On returning to Dublin she assisted designer Chisato Yoshimi on *Deirdre's Sorrows*, two versions by W.B. Yeats and Ulick O'Connor for a series of performances at the National Theatre.

Mark Galione (Lighting Designer) Mark's designs in Ireland include works for Irish Modern Dance Theatre, Cois Ceim, Dance Theatre of Ireland, The Peacock, Gúna Nua, Hands Turn, Classic Stage Ireland, Barabbas, Holocaust Memorial Day at The Waterfront, Vesuvius, The Ark, Fishamble, Theatre Luvett and Barnstorm. For Gúna Nua and the Civic he has lit *Earnest*, *BFG*, *The Odd Couple*, *The Sunshine Boys*, *Thesis*, *Trousers*, *Little Red Riding Hood* and *Sk8ter Jack*.

Carl Kennedy (Music and Sound Designer) Recent theatre work includes: Music for *The Last Days of Judas Iscariot* (Making Strange Theatre Company); *All Over Town* (Calipo); *Ellamenope Jones* (Randolf SD); *The Comedy of Errors* (Abbey Theatre); Sound Design for *Only an Apple* (Peacock Theatre, with composer Conor Linehan); Assistant Sound Designer for *The Resistible Rise of Arturo Ui* (Abbey Theatre). Other theatre includes: *The Giant Blue Hand* (The Ark Children's Theatre, with composer Denis Clohessy); Music for *Everybody Loves Sylvia* (Randolf SD); *Phaedra's Love* (Loose Canon); *End of the Line* (Cork Midsummer Festival 2008); *Love's Labour's Lost* (Samuel Beckett Theatre, BAS Trinity); *Howie the Rookie* (Granary Theatre, Cork); *They Never Froze Walt Disney* (Cork Midsummer Festival 2007 and Dublin Fringe 2008); *A Man in Half* (Theatre Lovett, with composer Nico Brown); *The Shawl* (Bewley's Café Theatre). He was Sound Designer for *Macbeth* (Siren Productions, with composer Denis Clohessy) and Sound Co-designer for *Unravelling the Ribbon* (Gúna Nua, with composer Denis Clohessy). Music and Sound Design for youth theatre includes: *At the Black Pig's Dyke*, *The Crucible* (Sligo Youth Theatre); *Beatstreet* (Action Performing in the City in Konstanz, Germany); *Ideal Homes Show*, *Debutantes' Cabaret* (Activate Youth Theatre); *One Last White Horse* (co-designed with Ian Kehoe for Galway Youth Theatre).

Paul Meade (Director) Paul Meade is Artistic Director of Gúna Nua Theatre, and is a writer, director, and actor. From Limerick, Paul trained at the Samuel Beckett Centre, Trinity College, and later received an MA in modern drama from University College, Dublin. For Gúna Nua Paul has co-directed the award-winning *Scenes From A Water Cooler* as well as *Trousers and Taste* by David Parnell, and the Irish premiere of *The Real Thing* by Tom Stoppard. He has also directed *The Shawl* and *Positive Dead People* for Bewley's Café Theatre, *Translations* for Hands Turn Theatre, *Medea* for Threshold, and *Death and the Maiden* for Mirage. His work as a writer included *Trousers*, *Thesis*, *Scenes from a Water Cooler* and *Skin Deep*, which won him the Stewart Parker Trust Award. He has also translated the plays *Stop the Tempo*, *All These Guys* and *Our Father Who Art in the Supermarket*. Most recently he wrote *Mushroom* for Storytellers Theatre Company, and wrote and directed *Meltdown* for Gúna Nua. Paul is currently under commission from Gúna Nua and the Irish Council for Bioethics.

Elaine Murphy (Writer) Elaine is an actress and writer from Dublin. As an actress she has appeared in *Becoming Jane*, *Boy Eats Girl*, and for RTÉ *Prosperity*, *The Clinic* and *Pure Mule*. She recently wrapped filming on the romantic comedy *Happy Ever Afters*. Her debut play *Little Gem* premiered at the Dublin Fringe Festival in 2008 where it picked up the Fishamble New Writing and Best Actress award. It was also nominated for Best New Play and Best Actress at the Irish Times theatre awards. She was awarded the BBC Northern Ireland Drama Award for 2009 from The Stewart Parker Trust. Her latest play *Ribbons* was commissioned by the Abbey Theatre for The Fairer Sex, a series of short plays from leading female playwrights.

GÚNA NUA THEATRE COMPANY

'A perfect example of a company that has embraced innovation'
Sunday Tribune

Gúna Nua Theatre is an independent theatre-production company based in Dublin, Ireland. The company has a strong commitment to devising and producing new Irish writing and presenting radical interpretations of classic plays. It has established a reputation for innovative, vital and exciting theatre which has received an overwhelmingly positive response from audiences and critics alike. Founded in 1998 by Paul Meade and David Parnell, Gúna Nua has received numerous awards and nominations for its ground-breaking work, and is now firmly established on the Irish theatre landscape. Previous productions include *Four Storeys* (1998), *Scenes From A Watercooler* (Winner, Dublin Fringe Festival Awards, Best Production and Best Actor), *Taste*, *Skin Deep* (Stewart Parker Award for Best New Play and nominated for 2 Irish Times/ESB Theatre Awards), *Thesis* and the hit comedy *Trousers* in association with the Civic Theatre (Dublin and New York), and the highly successful co-production with Plan B, *Unravelling the Ribbon*. Gúna Nua is grant-aided by the Arts Council and Dublin City Council and has toured extensively around Ireland, Scotland and the US. 2008 saw Gúna Nua productions presented in Romania and Serbia. In 2009, *Skin Deep* premiered in Philadelphia, followed by the world premiere of *Meltdown*, produced in association with Axis, Ballymun at the Dublin Fringe Festival.

'One of Ireland's most original, even radical, companies'
Sunday Times

CIVIC THEATRE TALLAGHT

The Civic Theatre opened its doors in 1999 and has consistently mounted an artistic and challenging programme of contemporary and classical Irish and international work in theatre, dance, opera and music for the community of South County Dublin, for the wider population of the city and the surrounding counties.

Although primarily a receiving venue for professional productions, the Civic Theatre produces and tours its own shows and has developed a successful co-production strategy with non-venue-based companies, as well as mentoring young theatre professionals by offering training opportunities on their in-house productions and co-productions.

Little Gem is the fifth collaboration between the Civic and Gúna Nua.

AUTHOR'S NOTE

When you start out writing, people always say: 'Write about what you know.' Being an actress for the last couple of years, I always had a yearning to write something myself. Decent parts are thin on the ground and I rarely recognised any of the women portrayed on the stages in front of me.

I work part-time in a women's health organisation. *Little Gem* grew from there, it's a mishmash of all the women I've met over the years: hardworking, not particularly rich or poor, ignored by the Celtic Tiger, and the recession probably won't make much of a difference to them either, you know, women like us, getting on with it.

I knew from my first meeting with Paul Meade and David Parnell in Gúna Nua that *Little Gem* would be in good hands. It's been a wonderful experience for me and I'd like to thank Paul for all his brilliant work and patience over the last year. I'd also like to thank our cast and crew, John O'Brien, Bríd Dukes and all the staff at the Civic Theatre, Pat Talbot for his guidance in earlier drafts, my fantastic family and friends for their unwavering support and finally to Gav, whose constant badgering got this play finished and the next one started – you're the best…

Elaine Murphy

Gúna Nua Friends 2009
Garry Burke, Maeve Binchy and Gordon Snell, Terry Clancy, Andrew Conlan Trant, Brian Friel, Aisling Meade and Cormac Gahan, Ann Hartnett, Mary and Michael Hennessy, Finola and David McKevitt, Liam and Eileen Meade, Noirin Meade, Ryan Meade, Kathryn Raleigh and Colin D'Arcy, Elizabeth Sheridan, Heber and Mary McMahon, Priscilla Robinson, Tim O'Malley, Ivan Graydon, Tom and Joan Meade, Marie Cummins, Mary Delaney, Bríd Connolly, Brody Sweeney and Clare O'Dea. A special thank you to all the other friends who have supported our work so generously since 1998.

If you want to become a friend of Gúna Nua and subscribe to our newsletter you can do so at **www.gunanua.com**

Gúna Nua Board
Garry Burke (Chair), Sheila Campbell, Catherine Deane, Michael Hennessy, Brian Motherwell, John Murray, Kathryn Raleigh

Gúna Nua Thanks and Acknowledgements
Eugene Downes, Madeline Boughton and all at Culture Ireland; John O'Kane, Jocelyn Clarke and all at the Arts Council; Kent Lawson and Carol Tambor for the Best of Edinburgh Award; Carol Ostrow, Sherri Kronfeld and all at The Flea Theatre in New York; Bianca Moore, Petra Hjortsberg, and Medb McKevitt; Cathy Belton and Jacinta Byrne and a big thank you to the great Jack Gilligan.

LITTLE GEM

Elaine Murphy

Characters

AMBER, *eighteen/nineteen*
LORRAINE, *late thirties/early forties*
KAY, *early/mid-sixties*

This text went to press before the end of rehearsals and so may differ slightly from the play as performed.

ONE

Amber

Jo's head is hanging out the window as the Hummer pulls up to the kerb. Thank God, I thought we were never going to get out of here with the amount of bleedin' paparazzi. The neighbours are all jammed into the living room having a drink, cos they've nothing better to do on a Wednesday night. They think my dress is massive, my false tan looks real natural and my hair is holding up lovely. In fairness I doubt a hurricane could move it, there's that much spray in it. Let a roar at my ma. She's sewing on the orchid Paul brought me, but missed the strap and got my chest instead. My nanny's over now, dabbing the spot of blood away with a tissue. They're all wrecking my head, pulling out of me. Tell me ma, I just saw Marian's little one squash an egg mayonnaise sandwich down the back of her new leather sofa. She's gone like a hot snot, armed with a J Cloth and Cillit Bang. The neighbours keep asking who my fella is… That's the one good thing about tonight; everyone finally gets to see Paul. I swear, I think my ma was starting to wonder if he existed at all. He turned around the other week and said he wasn't going. Thinks 'The Debs' is a rip-off; his one last year was shite. Nearly knocked him out. Who else was I supposed to ask, two weeks before? Anyone half-decent was already going. He looks deadly though. All the other spa's will be wearing tuxes and cummerbunds, but he's wearing this massive suit with diamond studs in his ears. He's chatting away to my granda – well, more likely nodding away cos you can't get a word in edgeways with him and Paul probably hasn't a clue what he's saying anyway. Ask him to grab my bag for me cos he looks like he needs saving and I can't pick up anything with these false nails. My best mate Jo finally gets through the front door. The neighbours are all over her now, saying she looks gorgeous, but they're really looking for an excuse to get to the other side of the room. My nanny's after bringing out more sausage rolls and they're trying not to look like total hungas. Jo's da followed the Hummer in his Fiesta. She's giving out yards telling him to get the bleedin' camcorder out of her face. She asked our mate Dean to go with her. He thinks his Lotto numbers have come up. She's no interest. Lewis Lawlor said he'd go with Tania Keogh ages ago and she's hoping they both ditch their dates when they get there. Finally get outside and pose at the car for a few more photos. Jo's da tries to get in the Hummer with us but we push him out, enough's a-bleedin' nuff. He joins the neighbours and me ma on the path to wave us all off. My nanny and granda pull back the curtains and wave from the living-room window. Jo pours me a glass of champers and tells me it's the dear stuff – not that I'd know, I'm already a bit giddy from the couple of cans I had in the house. My ma is piking me out of it through the window: (*Mouthing*.) 'Go easy.'

Samantha and Robbie have been holding seats for us at the table. Feel a bit sorry for Robbie, he must be twenty-five and here he is dressed like a dog's dinner, feeling awkward as fuck around all of us. It was real handy having him around when we were in school, always buying drink and never expected the round back. Send Paul off to the bar – won't start stinging Robbie yet. Ask Jo what she thinks of Paul's suit, she says it's lovely but the earrings are a bit poncey. My eyes keep wandering over to him as he's waiting to be served. This tall blonde bird stands beside him and smiles. They obviously know each other because they start chatting away. She's leaning in to him, shouting into his ear. He's stepping forward pretending he can't hear her, but he's really looking down her top, checking to see if she's all wonder and no bap. Ask Samantha: 'Who's yer one?'

Jo nudges me, asks what's wrong?

'Indigestion.'

'Sambucas!'

Follow her to the bar at the end of the room. Skull three shots each, and are back at the table by the time Paul brings over our drink. Paul sits down beside me and takes a big gulp of his pint.

Put my hand over his and say: 'Thanks for coming.' He says:
'It's cool,' moves his hand, leans back into his chair and
watches three girls dancing on the empty dance floor.

Jo and me just did a line in the toilets. Feeling nice. The music
is thumping in my chest. Unce, unce, unce. Like this fuzzy
feeling, know exactly where I am but when I close my eyes I
could be anywhere. Head back to the table and Paul's gone
AWOL. Ask Robbie where he went, says he's not sure, maybe
the jacks. No sign at the bar either but sure, while I'm there, get
another Corona. Scanning, when some bird bangs off me –
'Watch it' – but she keeps going. Blondie swings a left into the
ladies'. Think I hate her, in fact I know it, so I follow her in.
She disappears into a cubicle and I wait outside. Out of
nowhere, Jo appears beside me.

'Alright?'

'Of course.'

Blondie comes out of the toilet. She looks me up and down.
Give her daggers. Jo pulls me into a stall.

'Amber, give over.'

'I wasn't doing ah'in.'

She gives me one of her schoolteacher looks.

'You can't hammer every bird Paul talks to.'

'Don't want to hammer every bird, just her.'

She drags me out. Haul Dean and his mate Lee onto the middle
of the dance floor and gyrate like a pair of lezzers inbetween
them. The lads are all over us like a cheap pair of jocks from
Japan – Henry Street, not the country. Can see Robbie and
Samantha at our table and all the empty chairs around them. Go
to hunt the bastard down but Jo grabs me back.

'Stay here and dance.'

So I do.

Lorraine

Yer wan… 'the wrecker' – is shaking out all the neatly folded polo necks and throwing them back onto the shelf. Don't even have that many on display, but in the space of two seconds, she's managed to make three shelves look like a storm just hit. Refolding as quick as I can but can't keep up with her. She's moved on to shoes, picking up every pair and dropping them on the floor until she finds her size. Surprised we have them; her feet look huge. Kicks them off, leaving them after her arse in the middle of the floor, moving straight over to cosmetics. Squirts hand lotion on her palm but doesn't like the smell and puts it back with the shower gels. Tries to open the mascara but it has a hygiene seal on it. Tell her: 'Use the testers, that's what they're there for.' Sniggers at me and drops it in with the eyeliners. Sticks a lipstick in the pot-pourri jar.

'Stop it!' I say.

But she keeps going, mixing everything up. Moves over to greeting cards and puts 'New Baby' in with 'Birthdays'. Drag the cards out of her hand and put them back in their proper place. Katarina, a Polish girl that works with me, comes over trying to persuade me to go to the staff room with her. But I can't leave; the place is in a heap. The wrecker picks up a gift bag and I let a roar at her.

'Can ye not just look at it?'

She's shouting at me then.

'Are ye serious? You can't be serious!'

Katarina's saying: 'The customers can look at whatever they want.'

The floor manager is over now, wanting to know what's going on. Katarina says I'm not feeling too well; she needs to bring me outside for some air. The manager asks the wrecker if she's okay. Wrecker says she's very shook up. Manager tells me to go upstairs to be dealt with later. As they're walking away, can hear her asking if there's anything she can do? Wrecker says if she got a voucher it might make her feel a bit better. The little bitch looks back at me with a sly smile.

HR bird calls me in. Pats a chair for me to sit, then walks around the other side of the desk sitting beside the big fella, Mr Grant. Even though I've seen him around for years, this is the first time I've actually met him. He's wearing a lovely pinstripe suit, the same one the dummy is wearing on the second floor. Opens his leather folder and spreads a few pages out in front of him. Checks my name tag as I sit down. Says my track record has been excellent over the past ten years but the last few weeks have raised some concerns. Would I like to explain what happened today? Not really, but since I'm here, suppose I have to. Tell him:

'*She's* always in. Never buys anything, just up-ends the place. She's been winding me up since the January sales.'

'Do you think she comes into the shop specifically to annoy you?'

'I don't think it, I know it.'

'And are you aware of any other customers who do this?'

(*Pause.*)

'No, I don't think so.'

He heard I went home during my lunch hour three times last week, could I explain why?

How the fuck does he know that?

'See, on Monday I thought Amber had left the hair straighteners on. On Thursday, thought I'd left the iron on. And on Friday I'd left the back door unlocked.'

'And had you?'

'What?'

'Left the door unlocked?'

'No.'

'I see.'

Promise myself to never mention anything like this in front of any of the girls again.

'Is there anything you want to share wiv us, Lorraine?' He says.

Afraid to say anything, don't want to stretch my mouth open wider to fit my other foot in.

'Are you sacking me, Mr Grant?'

Looks at HR bird and then back at me. Wonder if he's riding her?

'Not at all; is there something we should know about?'

Telling them fucking nothing, suits have a habit of using things against ye later on. They're waiting on me to answer. I'm wide to this pair.

HR bird takes a quick glance at him then clears her throat.

'Your father was quite ill last year…'

She smiles at me to finish the sentence like I'm in playschool or something.

'What's that got to do with anything?'

'Has he made a full recovery?'

She reaches across the desk and touches my hand. Don't remember the last time someone touched me, hugged me, or even bleedin' nudged me.

The tightness in my chest loosens a little bit and I burst into tears. I'm mortified but I can't help it. There's snot running down my nose and everything. Mr Grant hands me a tissue and says I should take some time off. Don't want time off, I'd do me nut in at home all day. Says he'll arrange for me to talk to someone instead. Gives me a card, tells me to make an appointment and says the company will take care of the bill. He's to go to a meeting and asks HR bird to look after me. She makes me tea and gives me one of the nice chocolate biscuits from the luxury tins that we're trying to sell off in the supermarket. I can sit here for as long as I need to. She turns away and starts tapping on her computer.

Kay

(*Sitting on a chair, wiggling around.*)

I've an itch, down there. Seem to spend most of my life in waiting rooms and here I am again, after swallowing every tablet, trying every cream and changing my washing powder that many times I've run out of brands. Sometimes, when it's really bad, I open the bottom window in the living room and rest my leg on the ledge to let a bit of air circulate. The doctor opens her door and calls me in. She's a nice girl, very young, foreign. Thinks the itch is stress-related. Have you ever heard the likes of it? She's going to refer me to see a dermatologist; it could take a few months for an appointment. Think I could be dead by then, but take the letter and thank her anyway. She asks how my husband is. Tell her he's on the mend. The consultant thinks with the right attitude he could make a full recovery. She asks how I'm coping – grand, there's no use complaining, nobody will listen to me. She says she'll listen. Tell her about his appointments, medications and his physio. She stops me.

'That is all very good, Mrs Neville, but you should take some time for yourself, you are not a young woman any more.'

The fucking cheek of her. I've never felt old until now. She wants to know if I get enough help. Who? How often? Lorraine is a godsend, I couldn't manage without her, and now and again neighbours drop in and sit with him.

'You need more help, Mrs Neville, you look very, very tired.'

Gem doesn't like having people in his house all the time.

She hands me another page with numbers on it and asks if there's anything else I'd like to discuss.

You know that denture ad on the telly, the one with the couple kissing in the car in the rain? My Lorraine always says: 'Ah, Jaysus, there's yourself and Da on the telly again.' Amber does be heaving. Tell this young doctor I'm afraid I'll never get the man in the car back. She looks at me, confused. He was grand in the hospital, brave. It was when they brought him home it all changed. He's not the easiest of patients. He was never one for telly and he gets frustrated reading. In fact, to put it mildly, he's a cantankerous oul' fuck. I don't mean to go down this road but sure, I've started so I'll finish. I'm dying for me bit. We've always been very *compatible* in that department, which is a miracle in itself, because by the time you get to our age you'd normally be lacing the cocoa with arsenic not Viagra. I know it's not the done thing talking about your sex life, but Jaysus, I'm the wrong side of sixty not dead. I haven't had sex in well over a year and it's killing me. She's trying not to appear judgemental but I can tell she's shocked because she's fiddling with her hi-jab. Take that as my cue to leave.

Meet Marjorie Burke from pitch 'n' putt in Lidl on the way home. The women in the club talk like fuck about her but I've always liked her. She can tell I've been crying and asks me what's wrong. It kinda slips out, like everything bleedin' else today. And fair play to Marjorie, she offers me a solution – which is more than I got from yer wan and she charged me fifty euro. She says to go into Ann Summers and get myself a Rampant Rabbit. She got one six months ago and wouldn't be without it. Little does she know she's just put a stop to all those face-lift rumours; the woman is glowing from good old-fashioned orgasms.

Bit nervous on the 42B thinking about going into Ann Summers. I'm wondering whether you have to untie the staff from some dungeon before they can serve ye or if they parade around in leather catsuits. When I get there the girl is dressed grand, even smart. Tell her what I'm looking for and she doesn't even flinch. 'Follow me,' says she, so I do. We go down the back, to the left. I'm trying to look all cool, ye know, but I'm mortified. She hands me this thing. I can't believe the size of it. I can only describe it like a luminous, pink, plastic towbar. It has ridges all over it, silver beads down the bottom and a little claw thing sticking out the front.

'What's that for?'

'Your clitoris,' she replies, as calm as you like.

'Watch.'

Turns the thing on. Presses it once and it rotates. Twice and it vibrates. Three times and the head swirls around, all over the place.

'This is the original Rabbit,' she informs me, 'but we also have a Deluxe version.'

'The Deluxe must do the hoovering,' I say to her.

She tells me they haven't quite perfected that model yet. Ask her if she has anything else, a little less… you know. Jaysus, if I brought that home I'd never have sex with him again, whether he got better or not. She seems a nice enough young one so I'm honest with her, the Jaysus size of the thing petrifies me. She hands me this green thing, which she calls 'the Kermit, a six-incher – no extras.' I've to try Kermit out for a while and come back to 'upgrade' when I'm ready.

TWO

Amber

Wake up in Paul's bed about eight, feeling like shit. Go to the
toilet, turn the taps on full blast and puke my ring. In work at
twelve, have to go home to shower and change. Anywhere else
I'd pull a sicky, but Jo's da got us the job. There's a cup of tea
waiting for me in the kitchen when I come out. Paul's on his
mobile ordering me a taxi. Have a sip and look at the two
snoring bodies on the sofa.

'Alright, angel?'

(*She nods*.)

But I'm not. Paul picks up a leg of chicken from a snack box he
bought at half five this morning and starts chewing on it.

'Deadly night, wasn't it?'

'Great.'

Stee and Granite turned up about one o'clock with great
intentions of getting their hole – but forgot they were ugly
bastards and ended up back here, watching *Scarface* and
smoking doobies. When they all started banging on about going
to Australia again I gave up waiting and went to bed. Jo says
until someone else comes along, I'm 'handy hole'. Nearly five
months later I'm beginning to think she has a point. She wasn't
impressed with me coming back here last night. Went a bit
psycho on her, think it was the vodka. I was grabbing ice out of
people's drinks and lashing them out of it on the dance floor. She
nearly had me out the door when he turned up, said he was only
outside smoking with the boys. She went off in a huff and I came
back here. Taxi beeps outside. Paul tiptoes out with me cos he's
no shoes or socks on. Taps at the window and slips the driver a
score. Checking his ID, he says: 'Make sure she gets home in
one piece.' He leans in the window and kisses me goodbye.
Smile as he hops around, freezing in his tracky bottoms and T-
shirt. 'I'll text ye during the week, see what you're up to.' He

says. Wave at him from the back window 'til he disappears. He doesn't know it yet, but this time I'm not replying.

Meet Jo in the canteen before we start our shift. She says I look bollixed. She doesn't look the Mae West herself. Feel myself heaving again and have to do a Sonia to the nearest jacks. Mandy from accounts is in the next toilet.

'Ye alright?'

'Grand.'

Open the door; she's waiting at the sink for me with a handful of tissues.

'What were you up to, you look wretched.'

Don't mention the coke I did with Jo, or the spliffs I had with Paul and his mates. She kind of looks on me and Jo like little sisters.

'My hangovers are brutal lately.'

Stick my head out the window. (*She breathes in big mouthfuls of air.*)

'Hope it's not morning sickness.'

(*Pause.*)

'As if, have to stop mixing me drinks, is all.'

'Buzzing off ya – (*Laughing like a sheep.*) Mee-hea, mee-hea, meaaaaaaaaaa!'

She could put ye through a window, the bleedin' width of her. She sounds like a sheep on speed. My head. She finally goes, passing Jo at the door.

'Jaysus, and I thought the other one looked ropey.'

Jo's still huffy with me for legging it last night. Can't be dealing with her humours right now. Ask her to cover for me while I run out to the chemist. When I get back she's in the exact same spot, holding her hair back, swaying over the sink. She sees the brown paper bag.

'I'd plugs with me.'

Show her the test. Her eyes nearly drop out of her head. She's following me into the jacks. I'm like, 'Hello?' She says when we're out I always go the toilet in front of her. Push her out the door, telling her it's one in the afternoon and there's no queue.

(She's sitting on the toilet now.)

In two minutes I'll get an 'accurate' reading. Imagine me being pregnant? Like, a ma. There's no way. Imagine Paul being a da! That's mad. Like, I know I've nothing to worry about but Mandy has my head doing fucking overtime. My yokes are always all over the place but... I actually can't remember when I got my last one. If I was... Paul'd have to... (*Looks at the strip*.) Oh my God, my heart. Negative. I knew it. Open the door; show Jo. The fucking relief. I knew it, but you know... Jo checks the box, then checks it again. She says it's positive. Give over, an 'X' means no. She turns it a bit and says: 'Plus means positive.' Bollix.

Sitting at my desk waiting for calls to come through. I'm on directory enquiries today for an English phone company. This fella rings in, looking for a cab firm in Hackney. He doesn't know the name of the place or the road it's on but it's definitely somewhere in Hackney, yeah... Do I not know it? How would I bleedin' know it? I'm about to start a search, but it feels too much like work and he's been real ignorant so I cut him off. Trying to remember when the fuck it could've happened cos in fairness we're always real careful. I've done three pregnancy tests and they all say the same thing.

There was this one night, when we got back to his gaff and I was wrecked. Was lying there waiting for the bed to stop spinning so I could climb aboard the night train. He was off somewhere – probably playing that fucking Xbox with Stee – then he comes in and starts nudging me.

'You awake? You awake? You awake?'

'Well, I am now.'

Was so knackered, did the starfish – you know – (*She stretches out her arms and legs and flails about a bit*.) decked out, no energy. He's going at it like a mad thing and I don't know… Must've nodded off – only for a minute, mind – cos then I heard – 'Oh shite, Amber, it's split! Amber! Amber! Amber!'

I'm like, 'What, what, what?'

'Were you asleep?' He says, disgusted.

'Nooo, I had me eyes closed cos I was getting really into it.'

'I might as well be into necrophilia.'

At that stage I could feel my headache starting so I just said: 'Fuck off.'

But the next day I said to me ma: 'Here, what does necrophilia mean?'

The look on her face was pure horror.

'What weird shit are you getting up?'

'Ah, nothing,' says I. 'Heard it on the telly.'

It must be really bad – like when they poo on ye or something. Maybe it's his posh way of saying I'm shite in the sack. He does that sometimes, uses big words I don't understand, bet the cunt doesn't know what it means either. We hardly made a baby outta that, did we?

Lorraine

Debbie and Katarina have bullied me into going salsa dancing tonight. They gave me plenty of notice so I couldn't make up any excuses. I'm not really one for going out. For the last six nights I couldn't sleep, thinking about it. Told 'the lady' about it at our meeting. She said even if I didn't go to salsa, I had do one nice thing for myself this week. Was hoping at the end of it she'd say:

'Ah, you're grand,' but she didn't.

Must be a bit of a mentaller because she gave me a prescription for tablets. They're supposed to calm me down. I've to go back and see her on Monday. So with two days left, decide the one nice thing I'll do for myself this week is go to salsa class – even though it doesn't feel nice, it feels like torture, but I won't tell her that.

The girls drag me to a basement nightclub in a hotel in Temple Bar. The full lights are on and I never realised how manky nightclubs are. The carpet is worn down, the dance floor scuffed by shoes and there are gobs of chewing gum everywhere. The smell of feet in the place is rotten. The teacher walks to the middle of the dance floor and claps his hands to start the class. He's curly black hair in a ponytail and big white teeth that were only made for smiling. His tight black trousers make his bum look like Leroy's from *Fame*: high and muscley. Carlos – is fucking gorgeous. Pressing play on a portable CD player, he shows us a basic step. Katarina and I try and follow. Debbie has a bloke partner cos she's a bit of a pro and there's only five blokes compared to about thirty women. For an hour we shuffle around a bit, stand on each other's toes, and by the end of it we have something that looks like a dance routine.

'Zas all for dis week.'

We all clap, like this – (*She claps like a flamenco dancer.*) because now we all have rhythm. The main lights go off and the disco lights come on. A small black fella appears behind the DJ box and Jennifer Lopez blares from the speakers. Some couples spin out onto the middle of the dance floor but most of them dive on the now open bar. Katarina wants me to hang around for one and legs it to the bar before I can stop her. Watching Debbie throw shapes with yer man and don't know whether it looks sexy or gagging, when Carlos appears by my side, takes me by the hand and pulls me towards the dance floor. Know this should be the whole 'nobody puts Baby in a corner' moment, but I wish he would fuck off. Try and wriggle my hand out of his, smiling, saying, 'No thanks,' but the more I wriggle the tighter he holds onto it. He's no intention of letting go so I follow him. He looks me straight in the eye and says, 'Feel,' spinning me around. I've already stood on his toes twice, so stop thinking about it and just go with him. He throws me around like a rag doll and it feels… fucking great. When the song finishes, Carlos slaps this fella on the shoulders and says:

'Niall, meet your partner. (*Winks*.) You two will sizzle.'

Niall is a baldy fella about the same height as myself. I swear, I have never seen so much body hair on one person and he's wringing with sweat. One quick dance later – 'I'm just getting a drink' – and leg it.

Katarina is at the bar waiting for me. Says she can't stay too much longer, her husband is on nights this week and she has to get home for the twins. Niall comes over and asks if I'd like to dance again. All I want to do is spray him down with Febreeze but Katarina says; 'Of course she will,' drains her drink and waves me goodbye. The music switches to a slower tempo and Niall moves closer into me. Can smell his deodorant – for all the good it's doing him – and his aftershave which is actually alright, kind of musky.

'You haven't been here before,' he says. 'I would've noticed.'

Didn't even know he existed until Carlos threw him at me. Lean my head on his shoulder, imagining he's Simon Le Bon. My cheek sticks to his shirt and when I lift my face there's an orange smear of make-up left behind. Go to the bar and order my fourth vodka and Diet Coke, even though I shouldn't because I'm hammered already. The night's going well. Niall seems nice but in all honesty I can't really hear a thing he's saying over the noise. Debbie wants us to go for a drink upstairs with her and David. Head upstairs to the bar, which is a bit quieter, and sit into a corner table. David and Debbie are not even halfway through their drink when he lobs the gob and they start gnawing the face off each other. Niall and I are making small talk pretending like nothing is going on beside us. He's recently divorced and has a five-year-old son. Tell him I have a nineteen-year-old daughter. He says I don't look old enough; I'm not near old enough. Asks if I'm married and I say yeah but the last time I seen him was seven or eight years ago. Why did we split?

'We married too young, he was my first boyfriend.'

His wife had an affair with his best friend. Knows now he wasn't paying her enough attention, too busy building up his business. Think his wife should have kept her knickers on but he seems happier blaming himself so I say nothing. Chewing on an ice cube when he kisses me. Nearly choke. He stops, mortified. Swallow the ice. Look at him for a minute, then decide 'fuck it' and go back in for a wear. Even though he's cleanly shaven I can feel bristly hair breaking through his pores and rubbing off my skin. Don't know whether it's the kisses or what – well, truthfully it's most likely the vodka – but I feel on fire. There's electricity in those lips. Want to tear off his clothes and feel his hairy sweaty body on mine. Everything I've been burying for these last few years comes back like a tidal wave. The main lights switch on indicating it's time to go. Asks if I'd like to go back to his, and his face goes red:

'Just for a coffee or something.'

'Yeah, I'd love to.'

We say goodbye to Debs and David, who don't even come up for air, they just wave their arms a bit.

Get a taxi back to Niall's, holding hands in the back like a pair of teenagers. Can't believe I'm doing this. Haven't done it in years and years. And I know I should be nervous and freaked like I am about everything else, and I am, but I'm doing it anyway. Have nice knickers on because I always match them to my bra anyway, so that's all sorted. And I couldn't give a shite about my cellulite or anything else, it's not as if I'll be seeing him again. All I want is a break from myself for a few hours.

Get to his apartment. It's one of those new ones off the M50 somewhere. It's small but it's decorated minimalist so it gives the illusion of a bit of space. He cracks open a bottle of wine and I don't have the heart to say I don't like it, so have a few sips. Puts on some music and all of a sudden feel very sober and nervous. But when he sits beside me and kisses me again, all I can think is: 'Nice one!' Things get steamy on the sofa. Asks if I'd like to move to the bedroom, gets embarrassed, as if every time he presumes something he's insulting me. He's not! Drag him into the next room. Turn on the light and it's painted in bright rainbow colours, with a car bed and toys everywhere. Think it would take me two minutes to clear all them toys away and give the place a quick bang of a hoover. Just about to reach for Scooby Doo when he leads me into the opposite room. Opens my blouse, unzip his trousers, we fall onto the bed. Trying not to think about all that Lego in the middle of the floor. Both jump under the covers and as I'm pulling off his boxers, he says: 'Wait.' And I stop. My feet touch off his. He still has socks on so I reach under and pull them off. He's on top of me now. Ask if he has one of 'them things'. He does. Puts it on, lies back down. Don't remember it being this squishy. If memory serves me correctly it should be 'rock' by now. Niall nuzzles his head into my neck and I feel him shudder. This can't be it. It is it.

'I'm sorry, I can't.'

Well, thank the Lord for that because I thought we'd done it already. But now I'm paranoid thinking why the fuck can't ye? He gets up and goes to the bathroom. Lie there wondering what the fuck do I do now? – Get out. Must think I'm such a slut; nearly raped the poor fella! Grab my clothes from the far-flung corners of the room and get dressed quicker than I've ever dressed in my whole life. Hear the toilet flushing as I close the front door.

Kay

Doorbell rings. Unusual for this time on a Sunday morning. It's
only Amber; too lazy to go rooting for a key down the bottom
of her bag. Watch her mooching around the kitchen as I'm
cooking the breakfast. Says she doesn't want anything, her
stomach is at her. Tell her if she laid off them sambucas she
might get through a Sunday without Solpadeines. Says she
stayed in last night, she's not sick, she's pregnant. (*Beat*.) She
hasn't told Lorraine yet. Seemingly, she crawled in at two this
morning and still hasn't surfaced. At this hour on a Sunday,
Lorraine's usually halfway through washing the downstairs
windows. My itch flares up and I move around, trying to walk it
out. Amber's looking at me funny, saying: 'Ye alright, Nan?'
There's a roar from the living room. He's a fuck for ear-
wigging. Amber goes into the living room and cuddles up
beside him. Tell them I'm running to the shop for milk. I'm
really going out for a cigarette, even though I haven't smoked in
nearly twenty years. Walking down to Spar trying to keep the
tears in my eyes but it's no use, they're falling down my cheeks
anyway. I'm wondering what brand I'll get, the ones I always
smoked or these new 'light' ones? Lorraine and I gave up
smoking when she was pregnant on Amber and I think it's very
ironic that it's Amber making me go back on them. I remind
myself how bad they are for ye but then again I was off them
eight years and I still got breast cancer. They removed the lump,
had radium and the whole lot. Thank God now it's been all clear
since. Frightened the shite out of me though. From then on I
made sure we looked after ourselves properly. Made little
changes – ye know, bought wholegrain bread instead of batch,
Flora instead of butter, fry-ups only on a Sunday morning and
even then I'd grill everything. Ten years later nearly to the day,
Gem had his stroke. Never smoked a day in his life. Wasn't
overweight or anything, always running around doing
something. All our clean living didn't change a thing.
Hereditary, the doctor said. Happens. Some days the medication
turns him into a stranger. Them days, horrible thoughts run

through me head. Don't understand how they even creep in, cos underneath it all he's still my Gem. From the first day I saw him I knew. He didn't, but I did. He was a mechanic in the laneway near the factory where I worked. Every Friday – pay day – we went to Flanagan's, on the corner. He was going out with one of the other girls from the job. She was doing a line with someone else on the sly, and one Friday she went off to meet your man instead of Gem. Thought, right, if I don't go over there and talk to him now, I never will. So I did. Once we started you couldn't shut us up. He walked me home and asked me to the pictures the next day. When I went into work on the Monday, she was waiting for me. The girls told her we were all over each other in the pub. We were also spotted around town that weekend. Things were much smaller in them days; you couldn't go anywhere. She'd finished with the other fella that Friday. She went for me. I was an awful chicken. I ran. Ended up leaving the job but I kept Gem. Knew a good thing when I saw it. And we've been lucky. Other couples that got married around the same time as us have long separated, or are living under the same roof not uttering a word to each other. Every time I hear a scrap of gossip about so-and-so, I lie in the bed at night, looking at the back of his head, thanking me lucky stars we're doing grand. I always said 'I'd die' if anything happened to him, but I do actually feel like parts of me are slowly fading away.

Now Amber's pregnant and Lorraine's off seeing head-doctors because she can't cope. After Ray left she was grand, too grand for everything he put her through. And when her daddy got sick she put all her energy into making him better. Think she's realising nothing she does will make this any better. Before, I would've caught her, ye know… but I haven't got the energy any more. Feel like my little family is falling apart. Ask Jackie for ten John Player Blue and a litre of low-fat milk. He's a really happy Chinese fella. His name isn't Jackie but that's what the kids call him and he answers to it. He tells me they don't sell tens any more, he'll give me the twenty instead. Hand him five euro. Laughs at me, saying it's a long time since I've bought cigarettes. Tells me it's nine-something for them and the milk. I only want the one but it's twenty or nothing. I'll leave them, so. Walking out when he calls me back and hands me a Marlboro Light from his pocket.

'I've no matches,' I say.

In his best Dublin-Chinese accent he says to me:

'Jaysus, Kay, what do you want me to do – smoke it for you?'

Can't help but smile at him:

'Yeah, smoke it for me, Jackie.'

THREE

Amber

My nanny's sent me home to tell to me ma. Called into Jo on the way so she could come back to mine and be a witness if *someone* tries to murder me. They didn't even bother ripping me out of it, said it was a bit late for all that now. Sitting on my bed crying, when me ma walks by and asks what's wrong?

'*Nothing.*'

Slam the door in her face. She calls me a moody little bitch and corners Jo on the landing.

'What's gotten into her?'

Jo says she hasn't noticed. Decide I'll tell her *after* we go to the cinema, cos there's no point ruining the whole night. We're walking out the front door when me ma calls me into the living room and tells me to 'sit'. There's something up, she's not stupid – spit it out. Jo and me look at each other and together, I say, 'Nothing,' and Jo says, 'Tell her.' Me ma is starting to panic now, shouting:

'Well, someone better tell me.'

Jo is staring at me, making it real obvious there's something to actually tell. 'Come on, Amber, just say it.'

She gives me her fucking schoolteacher stare again, then turns to me ma, real matter-of-fact, and says: 'Amber's pregnant.'

Can't believe she just said that. I'm gonna thump her. Mouthpiece, we are so finished after this.

'For who?'

'Paul.' I say.

'Paul, that bloke you're always texting but the rest of us hardly know?'

And when she says his name she makes this real funny face. Don't know whether it's nerves or what but get a fit of the giggles. Me ma's losing it now.

'What has Paul to say about all this?'

Jo gets up to go but she's not going anywhere without me.

'You are going nowhere, lady,' me ma says.

'I am – the pictures.'

Jaysus, the hysterics out of her you'd swear she was the one pregnant.

'Amber, we have to talk about this; I'm ringing your nanny.'

As I'm closing the door I can hear her on the phone. She'll flip when she finds out me nanny already knows. I'm going to have a baby. A baby. I'm so fucked.

The gaff is spotless when I get home. Now normally it's real tidy anyway, but you know something's up when the smell of Silvo hits you in the hall, at twelve o'clock at night.

'Do you want to keep it?' she says from the kitchen.

Don't know, don't know how it happened in the first place. She says she's a fairly good idea. Agree to go to the doctor with her the next day. Sit there in silence as she irons tea towels. We never really talk. Don't know why I expect it to be any different now. Try to think of something to say. Like: 'I'm sorry for letting you down,' or 'Fucking hell I'm scared shitless,' but nothing comes out. She thinks I'm a waster, like me oulfella. She unplugs the iron and wraps the cord tightly from hand to elbow before putting it away. Stops at the door but thinks the better of it and goes on up the stairs to bed.

The doctor's asking if everything is all right with me granda, when me ma says we're here for me, she thinks I'm pregnant. I've done three tests, all positive. The doctor wants to know when I had my last period. This is the big question – can't remember. Never pay much attention to them anyway because they're always all over the place. And then a girl in work told me about her sister, who started ashtanga yoga, dropped to six-and-a-half stone and stopped getting periods altogether. Thought that was after happening to me. The doctor looks at me and says:

'Because you started doing yoga?'

And I say no, because I got that exercise DVD with your woman from *Coronation Street*. You know the way it says at the beginning: 'Consult your doctor.' When I didn't get my period I thought it was a side effect. Me ma's sinking down in the seat. Doc says the only way to see how far this is gone is by getting a scan. She writes me a letter for the Rotunda. Asks if I'm sure I want to go through with this? Yeah, dunno, think so. Walk me ma back to Mary Street, then head back to work. Phone Paul on the way. Tell him to pick me up at seven; we have to talk. He says it sounds serious. It is.

He's waiting for me near the front door, parked on double yellow lines with the engine still running.

'Where do you want to go?' he says.

'Nowhere.'

Shitting myself now, this is all starting to get very real.

'Don't know how to say this, so I'll just come out with it.'

'Before you start, you're doing the right thing.'

Look at him, like, '*What?*'

'Me and you,' he says, 'We're going nowhere, well… I am – Australia. Ah, c'mere. I'm cool with it; to be honest I was going to blow you out anyway.'

'You were? (*Beat.*) I'm pregnant.'

'You can't be.'

'You'd think, but there was that one time when it broke, remember?'

(*Pause.*)

'Nice try… I didn't even… ye know, that night.'

'Paul, I haven't been with anyone else, I swear.'

'Out.'

He reaches over me and opens the car door.

Lorraine

Had my meeting with 'the lady' this morning. Was horsing the mints out of it all the way up Baggot Street but don't think it made any difference; the bang of drink of me was still brutal when I went in to see her. Sneaked back downstairs last night after Amber went to bed and drank a half a bottle of whiskey leftover from Christmas. Shouldn't be drinking with the medication but I needed it to knock me out. Hope 'the lady' doesn't think I'm some kind of alco. Told her how frustrated I am that, even now, I can't find the words to talk to my own daughter. I know it's not the end of the world, it just fucking feels like it. She went to my mother. Suppose it's a good thing, you hear all these horror stories of kids ending up in awful situations because they'd no one to turn to, but I feel like fucking – kicking her. We've talked about this stuff. I could've… I don't know… She could've come to me. But she went to her. She won't even deal with what's going on in her own house. The other week, my da asked me to sort out his finances for him… Me ma wouldn't even discuss it. Sat on the couch with her head in the air, sort of wriggling around, ignoring the two of us. 'The lady' asked me how I felt about going through everything, and I said, funnily enough I felt proud of him. He hasn't made a fortune but he's been careful, and financially they'll be grand. We stopped then cos me hour was up. As I was putting on my coat she asked me if I did one nice thing for myself that week. Told her about *some* of my night out and how great it was and how I'm going to go to salsa class every week. Didn't mention it'd probably be a different class or that I kissed a sweaty bloke, even though I'm sure she'd agree it's great progress.

Since I did so well she says I can afford to do two nice things for myself this week. Think: 'Fuck her anyway, that's something else I have to worry about.'

Go into Tesco on Baggot Street to get a bread roll for me breakfast. My stomach is in ribbons from the whiskey and I'm afraid to eat anything else. Outside, I'm tearing into my Lucozade, when I hear: 'Lorraine, Lorraine…'

Look around but don't see anyone.

'Lorraine…'

Still looking around, thinking: 'This is all I need, to start hearing fucking voices,' when this bundle of clothes gets up off the ground. A big black Puffa jacket, tracksuit bottoms and ripped runners – which were probably robbed to order in a previous life – walk towards me. Recognise Ray underneath the woolly hat. He smiles at me. His teeth are so bad, he makes Shane MacGowan look like he has porcelain veneers.

'Was only thinking about you the other day.'

'All bad,' he says.

'Christina's anniversary is coming up.'

'It is.'

His sister Christina died in a fire years ago. Putting up the Valentine's Day decorations around the shop got me thinking of her, of both of them.

'How-wa-ye keeping?' he says, changing the subject.

'Can't complain.'

'Still as good-looking as ever, I see.'

And I blush, which is really embarrassing, because if anyone could see me blushing at this homeless fella they'd think I'd lost the plot. Ask about England, and what he's doing back, while tucking my handbag safely under my arm.

It's really taking its toll this time. He looks fucked; a stranger would add a good ten years onto his real age.

'How's Amber?'

'Pregnant.'

'That's great.'

'Well, it's not really but, sure…'

'I've seen her around Amiens Street, near where she works.'

Look into his eyes, the exact same as Amber's, and I ask him to do me a favour. If he does see her, will he just leave her and not say hello or ah'in. Maybe when he gets his shit together he can get to know her then. I've hurt him, I know, but I can't have him hurting Amber again either. Amber would probably tell him to go fuck himself anyway, she's subtle like that. He turns and saunters up the street. Still love his walk; it's such a cheeky swagger.

'Ray.' He stops.

'Are ye alright? Do you need anything – not money, now, like a sandwich?'

He smiles at me and just before he turns the corner, says: (*Smiles*.) 'Fuck off, Lorraine, will ye?' and disappears.

Kay

Take Lorraine's dinner out of the oven and put it down on front of her. If I don't have it on the table within a few minutes of her walking in the door, she'll start washing dishes and cleaning up like she always does, not that I've ever asked her to. You'd swear I never picked up a J Cloth the way she blitzes the place. Suppose over the years I've left stuff out for her to do, cos if I do a general tidy during the day she'll come in and start clearing out presses and cleaning the oven at all hours. She'd have the place torn apart on ye. She's a bit quiet in herself and I don't know whether it's over Amber or if it's these tablets they have her on. Say nothing; don't want to make her paranoid on top of everything else. Make us a cup of tea and wait for her to tell me about her day. She hands me an envelope. 'What's this?'

'Forms, for the respite thing.'

All I need to do is get Gem to agree and I can pack him off to the home for a few days. Put it down on the table, unopened.

'Mind your own business.' I say.

'You are my business,' she says.

Throws her eyes up to heaven and clears away the plates. To be honest, I'm getting a right pain in my arse listening to everyone's expert opinion. If I was to get rid of him, what does she expect me to do, go off and get a facial? Her new thing now is to do 'one nice thing for yourself this week'. Seemingly I should too cos I look wrecked. Sounds suspiciously like

head-doctor talk to me. She's been at me for ages, saying I need
to get a life outside him. Suited her, though, when she went out
to work and Mammy was there to mind Amber. So I haven't
been to pitch 'n' putt in a while, or down the baths for the aqua
aerobics, or on holidays, so bloody what? My husband is sick
and he needs me here. And I won't have anyone let him think
he's a burden.

FOUR

Amber

There are loadsa girls around me. They're all different ages and
colours and it's mad to think we're all going to be mas one day.
Told me own ma that Paul was coming with me this morning,
even though he's had his phone switched off all night. This
couple, a good few years older than me, walk out of the ward.
Yer one is no model or ah'in but she looks bleeding massive.
Her hair's all bouncy and shiny and her bump is real neat.
Swear it's like she's a light bulb up her arse cos she's glowing.
Her fella's holding her hand, smiling at her like she's the Virgin
Mary and wiping little tears away with a tissue. Want to run
after them and ask if I can borrow him for five minutes to come
in with me – but then a nurse appears and calls my name. Paul
walks into the room.

'Can't believe this is happening,' he says.

Can't believe he's here. He grabs my arm and follows the nurse.
She puts all this gloopy shite on my stomach and I feel it
churning but I'm thinking, 'Don't you dare, you little bollix,'
and it stops. She points Junior out with the nib of her pen.
That's our baby, it's about the size of my little finger. Want Paul
to grab my hand or look at his baby all googly eyed, but he's
pale and says nothing. Start sobbing. The nurse pats me arm and
says: (*Puts on a thick Cork accent.*)

'It's perfectly normal to get emotional.'

She says she'll be back in a tick, she's run out of gloopy stuff. Paul won't look at me, he's too busy staring at his hands.

'Amber... I'm not ready for this.'

'And you think I am?'

Grab the funny-shaped silver bowl and vomit. The nurse comes back in. She thinks I'm due around the end of June.

Jo says I have to go to our staff party tonight because they're paying for everything and since I'm not drinking she can have my vouchers. They've decided on Break for the Border cos it's one of those places all of us can go, the youngwans and the oulwans who think they're mad. I mean, Mandy is here and she must be thirty-one or thirty-two. Jo's told everyone I'm on antibiotics and keeps buying me West Coast Coolers, cos they're like fruit juice. They taste shite and I'm gagging for a proper drink. Just when I think I might get away with it, Junior threatens to heave so I switch to Coke. Buzzing off these Scottish fellas: there's twenty-two of them over for a stag party. One of them – Ian, I think he said his name was – has the hots big time for Jo. He's plastered and between the accent and the beer she can't make out a word he's saying. Can tell by her, though, she likes him. The groom's telling me about the hen party from Manchester they hooked up with in Temple Bar. They're mental. The girls are wearing devil horns and matching pink T-shirts.

The blokes are lining up to kiss the hen and after she chews the face off each one, she does a shot and everyone cheers. As she turns around I notice the back of her T-shirt says '*Samantha Swallows*' in big red letters. There's also '*Grace the Gobbler*', '*Sixty-nine Sara*' and '*Tantric Trisha*'. Now I know why the stag party are throwing the drink into them. The DJ switches from pop to eighties and you'd wanna see Mandy an' all, legging it in from the smoking area, doing that crap half-dance, half-run straight onto the dance floor.

(*'Don't Leave Me This Way' by The Communards is playing*.)

Herself, Jo and a few of the stag party are giving it socks.
Mandy's sticking out her belly rubbing her back singing along
real loud: 'Don't leave me this way...' Hate dancing sober.
Look like a sap and one of the stags is holding up me arms
shaking them around for me. These two young ones saunter
over – had they been lollipops they would've licked themselves
stupid. The blondie wan looks familiar.

She turns to me and shouts: 'They're playing your song.'

Keep sap-dancing, ignoring her.

'You don't know, do ye?' Blondie roars. 'Yer feller is going to
Australia on Wednesday.'

Everyone is listening to her cos she is shouting her fucking head
off over the music.

'Brought his ticket forward, he did, didn't want to be stuck with
yer little bastard.'

Like, how are you supposed to dance to eighties music, anyway,
I'm dancing like my oulwan.

'I know.'

'You did in yer bollix,' she says, breaking her shite laughing at
me.

Mandy freezes, her imaginary bump sticking out: 'Amber, I'd
no idea, I swear...'

I'm waving at her to give over, ye know, don't-be-stupid type
thing. The more of a scene she makes, the more the other girls
are watching me. All I want now is a fat frog, ten of them.
Grab the nearest thing to me and take a big gulp. It gets stuck
in me throat. Junior won't let me swallow it. Spit it out onto
the floor. Mandy grabs the nearest thing to her, which happens
to be Blondie's fake ponytail, and it comes out in her hand. Jo
wipes black tears from my face. Didn't know until then I was
crying.

'That mascara's shite' she says, grabbing my coat and leading me out the door. Want her to stay but she takes one look at them all swinging out of each other and she's adamant she's coming with me. As we're leaving, we pass Ian at the fire exit. He's snogging the face off '*Up the Crack of Dawn*' – the mother of the bride. I knew we shouldn't have bothered coming out tonight.

Lorraine

Got a call from a private number this morning. The only people who ever ring me from private numbers are people I owe money to. And even though I'd paid all my bills, I was still panicking as I answered. It was Niall. Think I would've preferred the repo man. He sounded really awkward and a bit posh. Defo didn't pick up on that before cos I would've slagged him over it. He was hoping I'd be at salsa last night but when I didn't show he asked Debs for me number. Wants to take me out to dinner, to start afresh. Fill him in briefly on the events of the last few days, now isn't such a good time. He thinks a night out could be exactly what I need. If I change my mind I've to ring back this afternoon. Hang up. Amber's standing behind me.

'Is that who kept you out late last week?'

Over the last few days I've been doing a lot of thinking. If I want Amber to open up to me maybe I should do the same with her. So I tell her.

'Some bloke I met at salsa. Wants me to go out for dinner with him.'

'When?'

'I'm not going, Amber.'

'Free dinner, Ma – so what if he's a spa?'

And I laugh at the way she makes it all sound so easy.

She picks up my phone and says: 'Go on, ring him back.'

Officially, this is my first date ever. Ray was my first boyfriend. Met him when I was fourteen. All we did was hang around parks and, as we got older, pubs. After everything I went through with him, fellas never seemed worth the trouble. Put on what I think is a lovely outfit, but when Amber sees me, she says:

'You look like Whitney dressed as Britney, go upstairs and cover yourself.'

Taxi arrives. Treated myself to one, cos I can't walk in these high heels and I've no idea where this restaurant is. Don't think I've ever been so nervous in my life. Amber walks me to the door and tells me to behave myself.

(*Rolling down the car window.*) 'Will I stay in with you?'

'No.' (*She pulls a sap face, closing the door.*)

Tell the taxi man where I'm going.

'Very nice,' he says.

'Is it?' Should've brought me pills.

'Ah, the restaurant is alright as well.'

Ask him to stop at a shop for me so I can buy an extra pair of tights. Not that I plan on getting them ripped off me or anything, just in case they snag so I've a spare pair. Queuing in the aisle when I decide to get another pair, because what if I was putting on the new pair and they laddered in the toe and it ran all the way up? Buy three pairs to be safe. Arrive early. Look for the toilet so I can fix myself one last time but Niall is already waiting at the bar. He looks really nice. His shirt is crisp and clean, not even a tiny bit damp. There's a vodka and Diet Coke waiting for me. Says he's delighted I came. Catch myself from saying: 'Unlike last week,' cos it wouldn't be funny, it'd be just mean. Sit down beside him and say: 'Tell me about yourself,' because that's what they say on the telly, that and my Xanax is kicking in. He tells me about his business and family and asks about mine. Tell him about my dad who's so ill, my ma who's so strong, and Amber who's so stupid, and how every night this week I've dreamed about breaking Paul Devlin's legs. Don't tell him about my junkie husband who stole everything I ever owned and broke my heart. Or the way I've gotten into the habit of locking every room in the house before I leave, or how I can clean until my hands are raw. Decide I'm going to do this right, which means keeping me mouth shut and my knickers on for the foreseeable future.

Kay

Dropped into Amber and the baby on the way home. Only six weeks old and he's already onto his third name. First it was Trey, but I called him 'Shelf' one day by accident and Amber went mad, saying she'd have to change it. Then he was Marshall after some rapper fella. Lorraine and I thought that was crap and harassed her into changing it again. Finally Lorraine suggested calling him after her grandad. Amber said she couldn't call the child Gem, he'd be battered, but we meant James, his proper name. Have to say it fits him lovely. Somehow he ended up with his granda's nose, which neither of the girls have, thank God. He's gorgeous, though, a little gem. And his granda is only over the moon. Going around calling him James Neville II and James Neville Junior. He's delighted to finally have another bit of testosterone in the family. Amber's already started calling him Jaime, which will probably be changed to Jay next week. Anyway, James is on the birth cert now, so it's staying. Wanted to drop in and make sure everything was okay with Lorraine being away this weekend. The Niall fella surprised her with a trip to Paris. She nearly died. Met him a good few times. He's a lovely fella, well-spoken. Very fucking hairy though.

Get home about two. Asked Nancy next door to pop in at some stage. He gets narky if I ask someone over to babysit, says he's not a fucking child, but sure you couldn't leave him on his own for too long either. Nancy is sitting in the kitchen watching *Emmerdale* on the telly. Ask if Gem's okay, and she says:

'Oh, perfect, told me to fuck off and watch that shite in the kitchen.'

Always marvel how Gem's speech is crystal clear when he's telling someone to fuck off. Go into the living room to see him. He's fast asleep in his chair. He's been sleeping an awful lot lately. The ads come on and Nancy heads off. Take the chops out of the freezer, peel a few spuds and dice a few carrots. I'll read for a half-hour while the spuds are boiling. Go upstairs to get my book. Searching around the bedroom when I notice the Ann Summers bag in the wardrobe. Kermit's still in his box. Never did get around to using him. Didn't like the look of him. He's like them Cool Pops Amber used to buy when she was small. Take him out. Switch it on. Listen to the hum. It's loud enough. Switch it off, don't want to wake himself. Suppose I do have a spare half an hour. I could... Just to see... like... Marjorie keeps saying it's un-fuckin'-believable. Hardly, though, it's an awful-looking thing. Lie down on the bed... I'm not sure quite what to do with it. It just looks so... The zzz... zzz... sound is putting me off. I'll put the radio on. Joe Duffy is interviewing some fella about his new book. Zzz... zzz... Ah... Joe Duffy's after putting me off even more. Back up, change the station. Q102. Love songs. Zzz... zzz... Gem'd piss himself laughing at this thing. Maybe I should check on him... zzz... zzz... I did take the chops out of the freezer that time, didn't I? Zzz... zzz... Better not forget that appointment we have on Tuesday. Zzz... Why are these things so fucking noisy?! Me bedroom sounds like a building site. Fling the thing across the bedroom. Zzz... It vibrates across the floorboards coming back towards me. Truth is, I can't cheat on Gem, even if it is with a six-inch piece of luminous green plastic.

Hear the faint tinkle of the bell downstairs. Put me alien willy away, promising meself I'll try again some other time. Thump down the stairs, the same way Lorraine thumped up them when she was a teenager. Open the living-room door and see Gem out of his chair, slumped face down beside the coffee table. Drag all thirteen stone of him to sit up. He's gasping for air and even though his body isn't moving, his eyes are darting all around the room.

'Hold on, love, I'll ring the ambulance.'

I know if I let go of him he'll fall face-first back onto the floor. I'm trying to hold him up, pulling him toward the settee to lean up against it. He's looking at me, trying to say something. I can't make it out. Those brown eyes are turning black.

'I yuv ye.'

'What love? I don't understand.'

'I yuv ye.'

' "I love ye", is that what you're trying to say, Gem?'

The head slightly nods and the eyes slip closed.

'No, Gem.'

I'm shaking him.

'Not yet, I'm not ready, Gem!'

He never listened to me once in forty-two years of marriage and he sure as hell isn't going to start now.

'Wait until I get the ambulance.'

But he doesn't. He lets one final breath and goes limp. Want to knock the shite out of him. He never gave up so easy before. I'm not sure what to do; so I sit there with him in my arms. It sort of feels like the old days, we'd settle down after he came in from football or whatever meeting was on that night. We'd always have a cuddle while we watched some shite on telly. Wonder what I'll do, now that I'm not his wife. It's all I've ever been or wanted to be. I should really ring Lorraine.

FIVE

Amber

Just got him down for his nap… Ah… he's fabulous, even if he does have my granda's nose. Freaky thing is though he's the absolute spit of Paul. Jo said most bastards are the image of their das, it's God's way of making sure they can't deny them. Asked her to be godmother, don't know why – if I died the last person I'd want Jaime living with is her. Wonder if 'down there' ever gets back to normal, or if I'll ever feel like a human again instead of a cow? Can't wait for him to get a bit older and buzz off him a bit, he doesn't really do much at the moment. Sleeps, eats, shits, cries, cries. I'm still wrecked, though, me ma's only gone since this morning and the house is in a heap already – but I won't be cleaning a thing until Sunday evening. Ah… she's been great but I needed a break from her as well. There was a reason I used to go out so much. Niall wanted to bring her away for her birthday but there was no way she'd go while I was still pregnant. So the other week I started dropping him hints. Fair play to him, he had it booked and paid for so she couldn't say no. He's nice, kind of quiet – real hairy. Had his kid up here last week, now he's a nutjob. Screams his head off at the slightest thing, wants bleedin' everything. Couldn't wait to see the back of him. Me ma's trying to be real patient but any day now she's going to let a roar at him. Having said that, she's in great form lately, haven't seen her so happy in years. It was mad seeing them off. Think the last time she was on holidays was when Nanny and Granda brought the two of us to the Canaries when I was about three. Niall called for her about half six this morning. Me and Jaime were up anyway so waved them off from the porch. She went to get in the car about three times but kept running back to remind me about something else. She finally gets in and is putting her seatbelt on when I get this awful pain right in the pit of my stomach. Not sharp or anything, like a dull ache, and I have this horrible feeling I should be stopping her getting on the plane. It must have been panic. Probably thought I wouldn't be able to manage on my own. We've been grand though; I've enjoyed having him all to myself.

My nanny was around earlier and she even said I was doing a great job. (*The phone rings*.) Bet you that's her, checking up on me. (*She ignores it, but it's persistent*.) Ah… fuck off. (*She finally gets up to answer it*.) Stalker.

Lorraine

The Metro is freaking me out. The only thing underground at home is rats and we're a bit too near the sewage system for my liking. We get to the green line, wait on the platform for about ten seconds and the train pulls up. Think it's a fluke but Niall says they're always this quick. Hop off at the last stop and follow the crowd up the escalator. Can see the blue sky as we move nearer the exit, the sun warms my face. Step on to the path and there, right on front of me, is the Arc de Triomphe. Look at Niall, like, isn't this the most amazing thing you've ever seen in your life? Imagine getting off the DART at Tara Street and having that right outside the door. Niall wants us to stroll down the Champs-Elysées, stop halfway for something to eat, then keep walking straight ahead to the Louvre. We're going to see the 'Mona Lisa'. The fucking 'Mona Lisa'. We're holding hands, popping in and out of shops, checking out the French DVDs in Virgin Megastore. He's been talking about bringing me away for ages but I wanted to be at home until Amber had the baby. The last holiday I was on was a weekend in Kilmuckridge. Amber had made her confirmation the week before, and himself wasn't long out of detox. The three of us were waiting in Busáras. Ray nipped to the shop to get few sweets for the bus. Ten, twenty minutes passed. The bus was about to leave and he still wasn't back. Picked up our bags to get on anyway but Amber didn't move.

'It'll be no fun, just the two of us.'

Walked around the corner and got a bus home. The minute we got in the front door, I told Amber to bring her bag upstairs.

Didn't want to be tripping over it in the hall. She put her bag up, then came into the kitchen and put two slices of bread under the grill.

'Me confo money is gone.'

I was about to launch into her, when she said:

'It was my own fault; forgot to lock my bedroom door. Do you want tea?'

Didn't say another word. She made the tea. The next day I changed the locks. Haven't been really pushed on holidays since then, probably why Niall ended up surprising me. Think my ma put him up to it. Collared me one day, told me to stop making him pay for things he hadn't done. He wasn't always going to be so patient, so quit acting the cunt.

We stop at a café with little tables outside and order a bottle of wine while we decide on what to eat. I'm getting a taste for the wine now. Niall says he's never seen me so relaxed. I know; can't wipe the smile off my face. He tells me to get out my phone, he'll take a picture and we'll text it to Amber for the craic. Turn it on and wait for a signal. I'm practising my poses for Niall – with or without the glass – and the phone beeps, one message after another.

'Somebody's missing ye.'

He picks it up and hands it to me. And I know, without even looking at any of them messages, my da's after dying.

Kay

Lorraine, Amber and I are looking out the tinted windows at everyone outside the church. They've been catching up with old friends, while waiting for the coffin to arrive and saying how terrible it is they only see each other at funerals. The car is cold from the air conditioning even though it's warm and sunny outside. Lorraine looks at me as if to say: '*Are ye right?*' and I say: 'In a second, chicken.'

Amber looks fed up. She's a pain in her arse with the whole day already. Know how she feels. There's something on her mind, I know by her.

'Are you alright, love?'

She kind of shrugs her shoulders a bit, 'Can I ask you something, Nanny?'

Brace myself for what's coming cos you never know with this one.

'Do you think he was just holding on until I had Jaime?'

Never let myself think about these things. Suppose I always hoped he was holding on for me.

'Maybe, Amber, I don't know. I do know he was delighted he got to meet him and when you called him James, well, he was chuffed with himself.'

'He wasn't disappointed in me, then?'

'Don't be so stupid, you could never do wrong in his eyes, you know that.'

Pull her over for a hug. Whatever I've said seems to work because her face isn't as cloudy-looking as it was.

Gem's brothers and their sons slide the coffin out of the hearse and lift it onto their shoulders. We follow them through the guard of honour. All the kids from six to sixteen are dressed in their stripey blue-and-white kit. Their white shorts are sparkling. Gem has finally gotten someone's mother to wash the bloody things. 'How-wa-ye, Kay,' some of the kids say as I pass, some are too upset to look at me. Jo is waiting at the church door with Jaime all snuggled up in his buggy. She gets a bit embarrassed because she doesn't know what to say. I don't know what to say either so I just say, 'How-wa-ye, luv,' and move on. They place the coffin on front of the altar and we all sit down. Feel like I'm at me own funeral. My family is here. Gem's is here. Fellas from his job, various committees, even parents whose kids were in school with Lorraine. Bet he's looking down; pissed off he's not able to go to the hotel for a few pints after. Niall sits down behind us and touches Lorraine's shoulder. It's nice to see her finally having a bit of happiness. The good ones are hard to come by. Remember my own mother saying to me: 'Gem by name, Gem by nature.' It reminded me to hold onto him tight. The service is nice. The priest goes on a bit but he's getting paid a few bob, it's the least he can do. Know I should be upset but I'm too nosy looking around to see who's here. The church is packed. Wonder if Gem can see all the people who want to say goodbye to him. At the cemetery the priest says a few more prayers but he makes it quick; it's coming up to two and people are getting hungry, myself included. When they lower his coffin into the ground I realise for the first time that's my Gem they're putting in there. All day I've been taking mental notes like I'm going to see him later. I'm not ready for him to go. I want him back, even the banjaxed version will do.

'What, Ma?' Lorraine whispers to me.

'I don't want to be without him.' I say out loud.

'I know, Ma, I know.'

But she doesn't know, she doesn't know. I've been Mrs James Neville twice as long as I was ever Kay Kelly. He hadn't even retired, for fuck's sake. What am I supposed to do? Sit around and wait twenty years until I eventually die and join him? Lorraine is pulling me away from the grave but I don't want to leave him. I am making a scene, I know. Can hear people talking and getting upset, others are just walking away.

Couldn't give a shite. I'm staying where I am. Amber comes over and hoists me up under the arm, the same way I did when she was small.

'You're not making a thick out yourself,' she says, dragging me towards the car.

Hold my ground. Lorraine's trying to break the two of us apart, hissing at Amber to stop. She eventually lets go and runs off towards Jo. Lorraine gently steadies me on my feet and kisses me on the cheek.

'We'll give you a minute, Ma,' she says.

Open my hand and stare at the soil. After a few minutes I slowly pour it into Gem's grave. Can't say goodbye to him, not yet. Turn around and follow them back to the car.

SIX

Amber

Jo, me and Jaime get a lift back to The New Hotel with Uncle Tony. Even though it's not the 'new' hotel any more, it's opened about three years. Head straight for the bar. Had to stop breastfeeding. It was turning me stomach. And I've had more than enough of being teetotal. Nine months of it I had, well seven... six and a half, really. My ma's going mad, said the baby needs it for his immune system. Me bollix, six weeks was loads. We're the only ones in the bar, except for a couple near the window. They're looking at me like they know me. Think they're friends of me ma's. Smile at them and they smile back.

'Amber?'

'Can we have a word with ye, love?'

Get Jo to follow me over with Jaime.

'We're Paul's parents,' yer woman says.

Jo is pushing the buggy behind me, hears the tailend of the sentence and spins it back around. Can't believe she's legging it, leaving me on me tobler with these two.

'Maybe this wasn't such a good idea, the day that's in it an' all. I'm sorry, love.' The oulfella says, getting up to go.

I'd heard Paul's ma and da wanted to see Jaime. I was getting around to it, but I had no idea how mental everything would be. A five-minute stroll to the shop now takes hours of packing before you even walk out the bleedin' door.

'You're grand, sit down.'

Don't know where this calmness is coming from, feel real mature or something.

'Knew your granda from years ago. Would you believe I played on the under-sixteens' for him?'

He takes out an old photo from the inside of his jacket and hands it to me. It's the 1974 football team. All the lads are wearing the blue-and-white kit, except all their hair is real long. My granda's wearing flares and has a beard. I've never seen him with a beard before. It's mad. Know this sounds stupid, but I've never thought of him as anything other than my granda. The oulfella says to hang onto it; he fished it out especially for me today.

'We saw the photos you sent Paul on e-mail, he's gorgeous, it's like looking at Paul all over again...' The ma says.

He'd rang a good few times all apologies, but I was having none of it. If he meant it, he'd be ringing from Dublin not Australia.

'Do you want to see the real thing?'

The oulwan is shaking a bit and the oulfella holds her hand. Shout for Jo to bring over the buggy and take Jaime out and pass him to his grandparents. He goos and gaas like never before and his eyes are wide-open staring the two of them out of it. His timing is perfect.

'We'll head off in a few minutes, love,' the oulfella says.

He's real nice, pity his poxy son doesn't take after him. Tell him to relax, finish his pint, if they want to hang on, there'll be soup and sandwiches going around.

A few more people have arrived. Me ma sits me nanny and me down in a corner before going to the bar. Show my ma the photo and she gets a great laugh out of it.

She wants to know where I got it.

Bring her over to meet them, since we're all sort of related now.

Jo appears with me drink.

(*Whispering.*) 'The fucking cheek of ye, sending pictures to Paul.'

'You wouldn't take his calls.' She says.

She's supposed to be on my side, sometimes I do fucking wonder about her. 'He's coming back next week, wants to be here for the christening.'

Can feel the anger in me rising, but then there's a tiny little bit of me, way way way down, that's bleedin' delighted. And now I'm raging with myself that after everything he's done, he can still make me feel this way.

Lorraine

Chatting away to Linda and Declan – Paul's parents, they seem very nice – when the hotel manager asks for a quick word. If he's here to get me to shut Uncle Tony up singing, he's no bleedin' chance. He's already sang, '*He's My Forever Friend*' twice and no doubt we'll hear it again before the night is over. But it's not that, there's somebody in the lobby who won't leave without seeing me. Me stomach plummets as I walk out the door with him.

Ray is sitting on a couch surrounded by three security guards.
He's in floods of tears, roaring at them to get their hands off him.
Calm Ray down. Explain he'll be fine. Just need to take him
outside. Grab him by the arm and lead him out the door into the
car park. A few friends and relatives are outside having a smoke.
I'm mortified. Can't believe he turned up here like this. Don't see
the fucker for years and now for the second time in a matter of
months. I'll give it to him – he could always pick his moments.

'Just wanted to say I'm sorry, is all.'

Know somewhere in his fucked-up little brain he's trying to do
right by me, show me he still cares, but not today, or here, in
front of everyone.

'I know what it's like to lose someone.'

And that's another thing. I'm so sick of his poor sister getting
the rap for every time he makes a fucking mess of things. He's
off his head, he'd have to be to think this was a good idea. Niall
appears beside me.

'Everything okay?'

This is not how I wanted him to find out about Ray.

The way Niall looks at me is different. No bloke has ever
looked at me this way before. I'm not a fucking loser to him.
I'm interesting and quirky, not mental and pathetic. I'm worth
wining and dining, and taking on weekends away to Paris –
even if we only get to have fucking lunch there. And I hate that
Ray has let him see this side of me.

'Who's this?'

Ray's tears have magically disappeared. He's actually
attempting to square up to him.

'Niall, Lorraine's…'

Ray looks at me.

(*Laughs.*) 'A fucking southsider, Lorraine? How could ye?'

He swings a punch but Niall doesn't even have to duck, it's totally off and Ray falls on his arse. Beg Niall to go back inside – I can handle this. If he goes, I'll get rid of him quicker. Niall doesn't say anything, just moves off to where everyone is smoking, and now watching, and keeps a close eye on me from there. Can see over Ray's shoulder that Amber's slipped out for a sly smoke. She's about to walk over when Niall stops her. He did right, if Ray saw her he'd get even more hysterical. Think he's let off enough steam and tell him it's time to go. He pulls himself together.

'I'm in trouble, Rainey, can't dig myself out of it this time.'

Knew there had to be some other reason to him being here, how could I think for one fucking second it was for me?

'I'm heading back to England. Tell Amber I said goodbye.'

He hugs me tight but I don't hug him back. My stomach churns at the stench of his clothes and the feel of his bony arms around me.

'Heard she'd a little boy.'

'Yeah, James – Jaime.'

Break away from him, breathing through my mouth. Look at him, trying to find a spark of the old Ray from before but he's completely gone. Know the next time I hear from him, it will be through a phone call from some copper.

'Bye, Ray.'

Walk back to the smoking area and thank God – again – for making me pregnant when he did.

'Are you okay, Ma?'

'Yeah, he was letting me know he's going back to England.'

Amber hugs me. This is the third time she's hugged me since she became a teenager. The first time was the night she found out Paul was leaving and the second time was when she went into labour. Smile at Niall over her shoulder. He's still looking at me that same way. He reaches out and softly touches my hair.

Kay

Promised myself I wouldn't get plastered today but I'm well
over my three-brandy quota, must have had at least eight by
now. My head is going to be splitting in the morning.
Georgie's son said he'd drive us home – tell him to round up
the troops, I'm ready to go. I was sitting on my own in the
corner for a while, like a child recovering from a tantrum.
Don't know whether it's age or what but I wasn't even
embarrassed about it. When people were sure I'd calmed
down they started coming over in dribs and drabs. They said
they were sorry. They don't know what to say. He'll be sorely
missed. It's an awful shame. The usual shite. Then something
lovely happened. A few drivers from the bus garage he worked
in tell me about the time he dressed up as Santy for the Family
Day Christmas Party. He told all the kids to ask for Man
United jerseys, especially if their oulfella supported
Liverpool. He used to collect the forgotten umbrellas from the
buses and keep them in a bucket near the office, so the girls
never got caught in the rain. His friends joined in. I never
knew they couldn't get him off the karaoke machine when
they went away to Portugal that time to play golf. That was
how the whole 'My, my, my Delilah' thing started on the
sidelines at the football matches. Didn't think he still talked so
fondly of me to the lads. How he didn't know it at the time but
he married his best friend, that we were 'great oul' pals'. His
brothers, Tony and Georgie, tell me how he nearly went off
the deep end when I found that lump in my breast. He'd never
been so scared in all his life. Don't remember him being
scared, I just remember him being there. You think you know
someone inside out, but even now after all this time my Gem's
still surprising me. I'm wrecked now. Can't wait to get home
to my own bed. Lorraine and Amber have been staying with
me the last few days and the place is like a crèche. For one
little person, Jaime sure has a lot of stuff. Amber does be
showing me how to hold him an' all, like I never reared one of
me own. Arrive back at the house and stick the kettle on for a
decent cup of tea. Amber and I have hardly a mouthful gone

when Lorraine swipes them off us to wash up. Head for the bed. Lorraine follows me up and helps me to get undressed. I let her. Amber comes into the room and says:

'Another few years, Nana, and we'll be changing your nappies.'

Tell her to fuck off and she runs out laughing. Lorraine puts me in bed and kisses my head. I'm finally on my own for the first time all day. Gem's stuff is still lying around the room like he just popped down the local for a pint. I upended the place yesterday looking for that dark blue tie he wears with his good navy suit. Can still smell him on the pillows and the sheets. Don't understand how so much of him can be still here. Must have been crying louder than I thought cos Amber is getting in the bed beside me. Didn't even hear her come in the room. Lorraine comes around the other side and bangs her foot off the locker. She's jumping around the room cursing the thing, holding her throbbing toes. Amber's cracking up. Look down at the drawer and see the head of my alien willy sticking out and slam it shut. Lorraine is getting narky with Amber, telling her to shut up, that it's not funny. This sets off Amber even more. Her giggle is infectious.

'Fuck ye,' says Lorraine getting into the bed beside me.

This sets the pair of us off again. Lorraine switches off the bedside lamp. Amber is trying to settle down but she can't stop herself giggling now and again. Her giggles quietly change into sniffles. Put my arm around her. Little Jaime starts crying in the other room. Exactly like his great-grandfather, wants to be in the middle of everything. Amber thuds out of bed and brings him back with her.

'You'll give him bad habits, Amber,' Lorraine says.

'Shurrup, Ma.'

'She will, won't she, Ma?' Lorraine says to me.

'Let her do it her own way.'

'Yeah,' Amber says, even though I know Lorraine is dead right.

We all settle down to sleep again. The girls snuggle in beside me. Listen to Jaime breathing softly in and out. Whisper goodnight to Gem.

'Goodnight, grumpy arse.'

Close my eyes, trying to trick myself into sleep on my first night without him.

The End.

A Nick Hern Book

Little Gem first published in Great Britain in 2009 as a paperback original by Nick Hern Books Limited, 14 Larden Road, London W3 7ST, in association with Gúna Nua Theatre Company and the Civic Theatre, Tallaght

Reprinted 2010

Little Gem copyright © 2009 Elaine Murphy

Elaine Murphy has asserted her moral right to be identified as the author of this work

Cover photograph by Dermot Kelly
Cover designed by Ned Hoste, 2H

Typeset by Nick Hern Books, London
Printed and bound in Great Britain by CPI Antony Rowe, Chippenham, Wiltshire

A CIP catalogue record for this book is available from the British Library

ISBN 978 1 84842 078 6

FSC
Mixed Sources
Product group from well-managed forests and other controlled sources

Cert no. SGS-COC-2953
www.fsc.org
© 1996 Forest Stewardship Council